ARTS & CRAFTS PRIMARY 5

Jane Martin

Art consultant:
Lissete Madrazo

Course consultant:
Harriet Thompson

BY ME

My name is:

....

....

....

Contents

Looking in detail

Artists carefully observe and study the world around them. They look for details in everything they see.

Children's Games, Pieter Bruegel the Elder. 1560

1 Look at the painting and find:

a. a boy climbing a tree.
b. a girl running in a red coat.
c. a boy standing on his head.
d. two girls carrying a basket.
e. three boys sitting on a fence.

2 Can you find these objects in the painting?

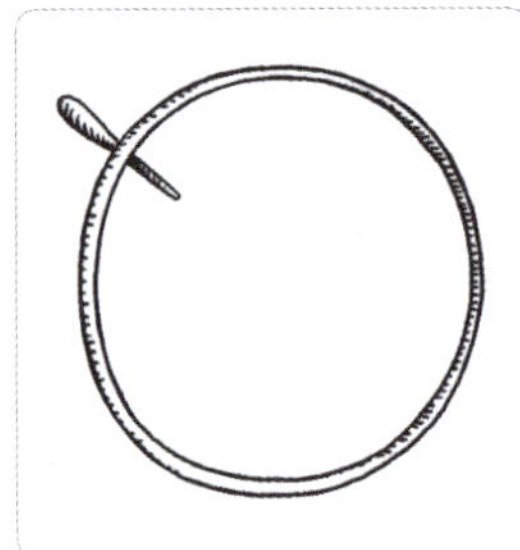

hoop

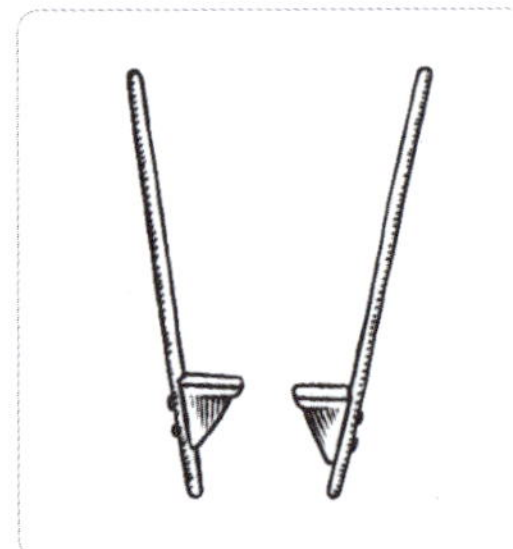

stilts

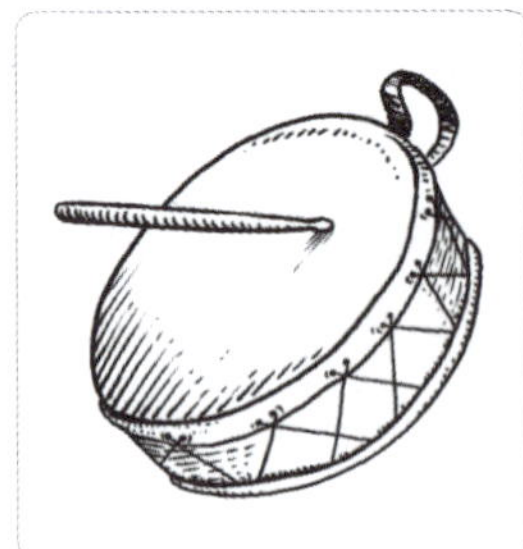

drum

doll

You can observe details like an artist. Make a *detail detector* and observe the world around you.

1 Fold the paper. Cut out a square.

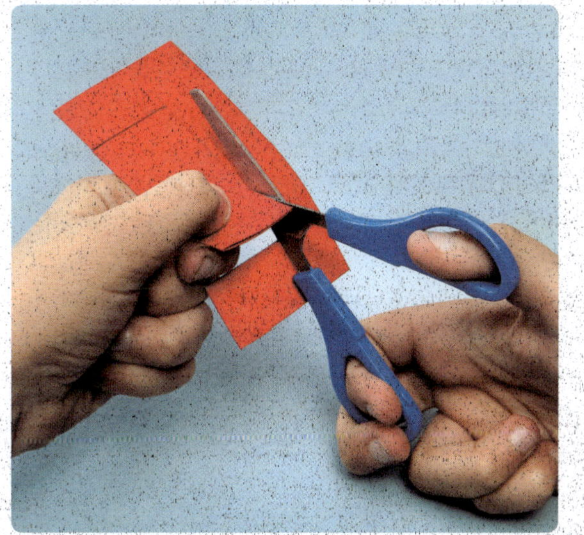

2 Observe. Draw the detail you see.

1 Friendly figures

Little Giants, Francisco de Goya y Lucientes. 1792

1. Why do you think this painting is called *Little Giants*? Use the words below to help you.

children	countryside	game	short	shoulders	tall

2. Read about how artists show people in their artwork.

Figures in Proportion

Goya observed people in everyday life. He often painted people, or figures, doing daily activities. In this painting we can see boys playing together.

Artists use the size of the head to show the correct proportion and shape of a figure.

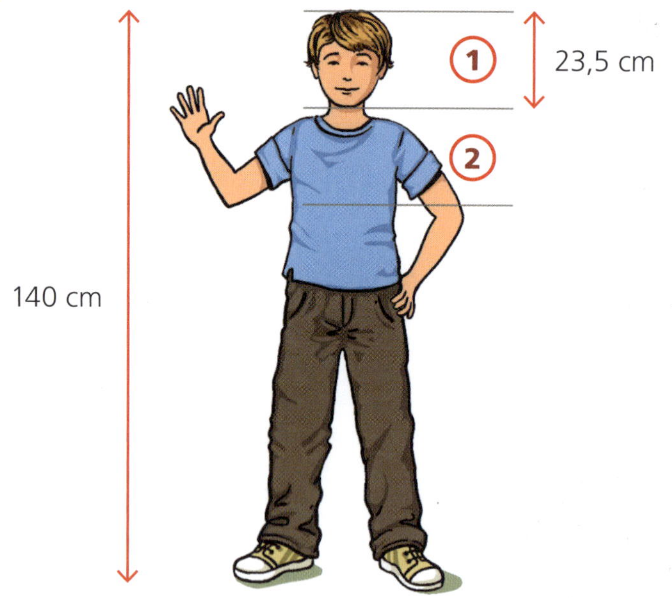

Measure how tall you are and then measure the length of your head. How many heads tall are you?

2 Activity 2

3 Draw a figure of a boy or a girl. Look at the example. Draw the head, the lines and the ovals. Finally, complete the figure and colour.

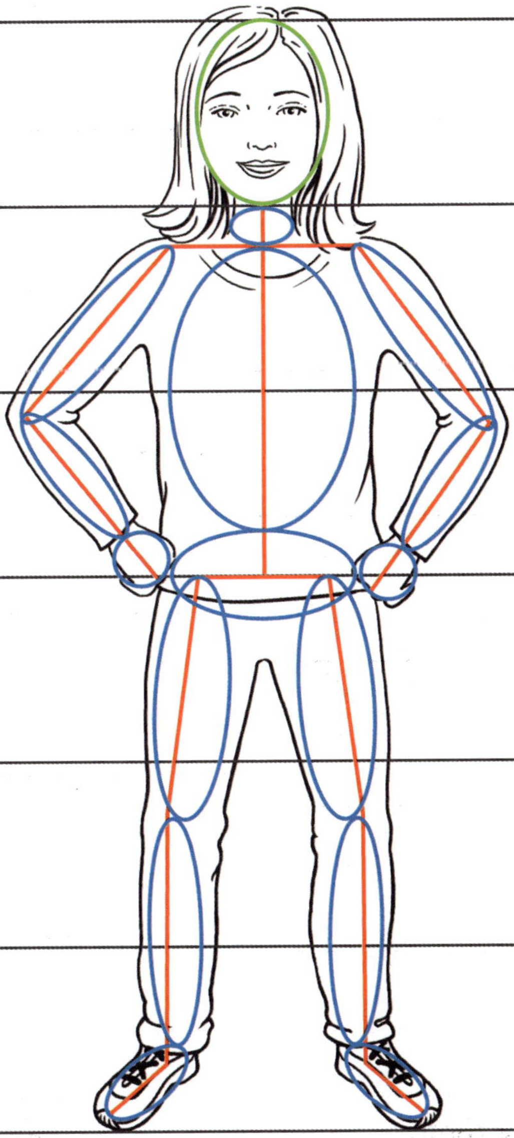

Watch me grow

As people grow, their size and proportion change. Artists can show people of different ages.

1 Complete the lines. Add the ovals.

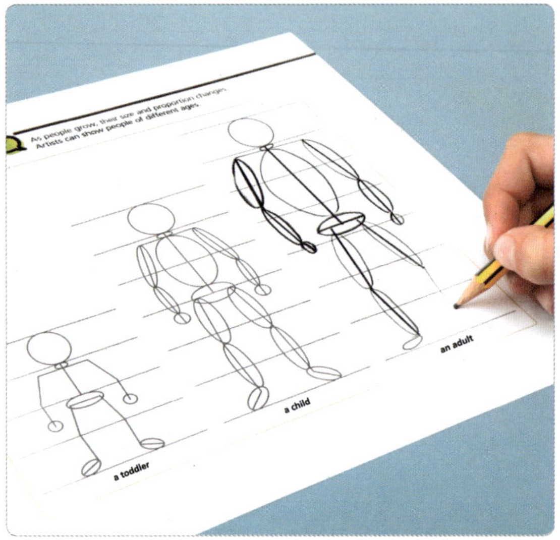

2 Complete the figures. Colour.

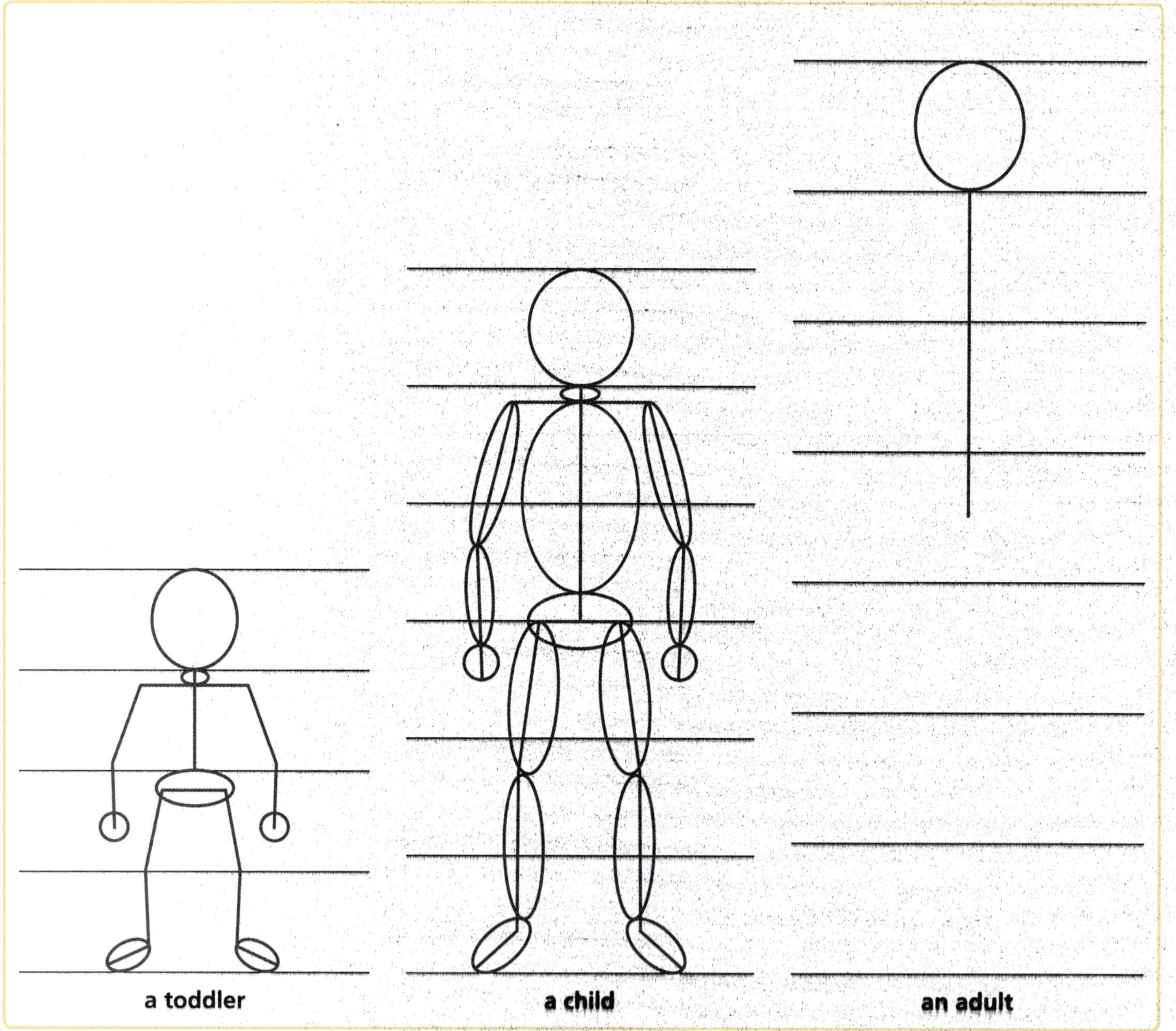

Figures all around

Some artists show friends and family in their artwork. They look carefully at the size and shape of the person.

Step 1

Observe your partner.
Draw lines and ovals.

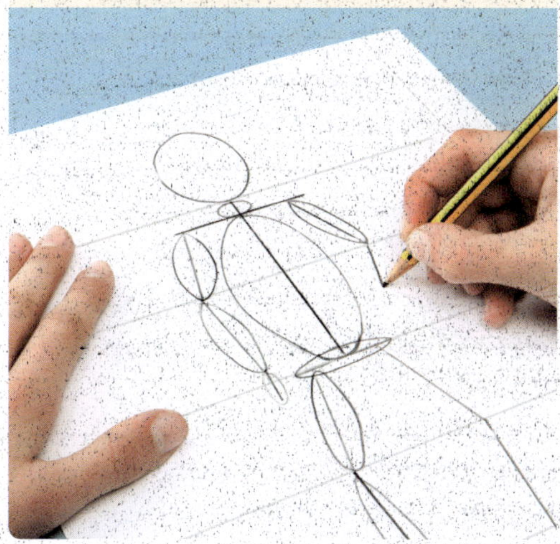

Step 2

Complete the figure.

Step 3

Draw their face and hair.

Step 4

Colour and cut it out.
Make a group portrait.

Template page 65

2 Exploring size

Ship in a bottle.

1 How do you think the artist got the small ship inside the bottle? Use the words below to help you.

bottle	cork	flag	sails	ship	string

2 Read about how artists show small objects bigger and big objects smaller.

Ship in a Bottle

This is a model of a ship. The model is much smaller than the real ship.

First artists measure an object. Then they make a model to scale. The model is equal but smaller.

Artists use scale to show objects bigger or smaller in many types of artwork, including painting and sculpture.

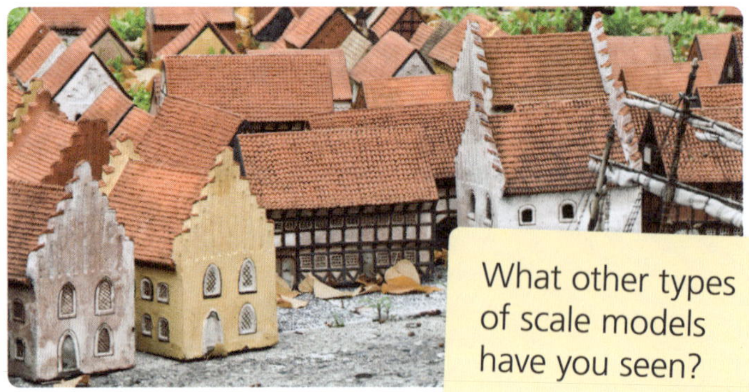

What other types of scale models have you seen?

3 Activity 2

3 Use the grid to draw the picture to a larger scale. Colour.

My treasure map

Scale is used to draw maps. Maps can show the size and distance of large areas in a small space.

1 Look at the key. Listen and draw the objects on the map.

2 Choose a square to bury your treasure. Write directions to your buried treasure.

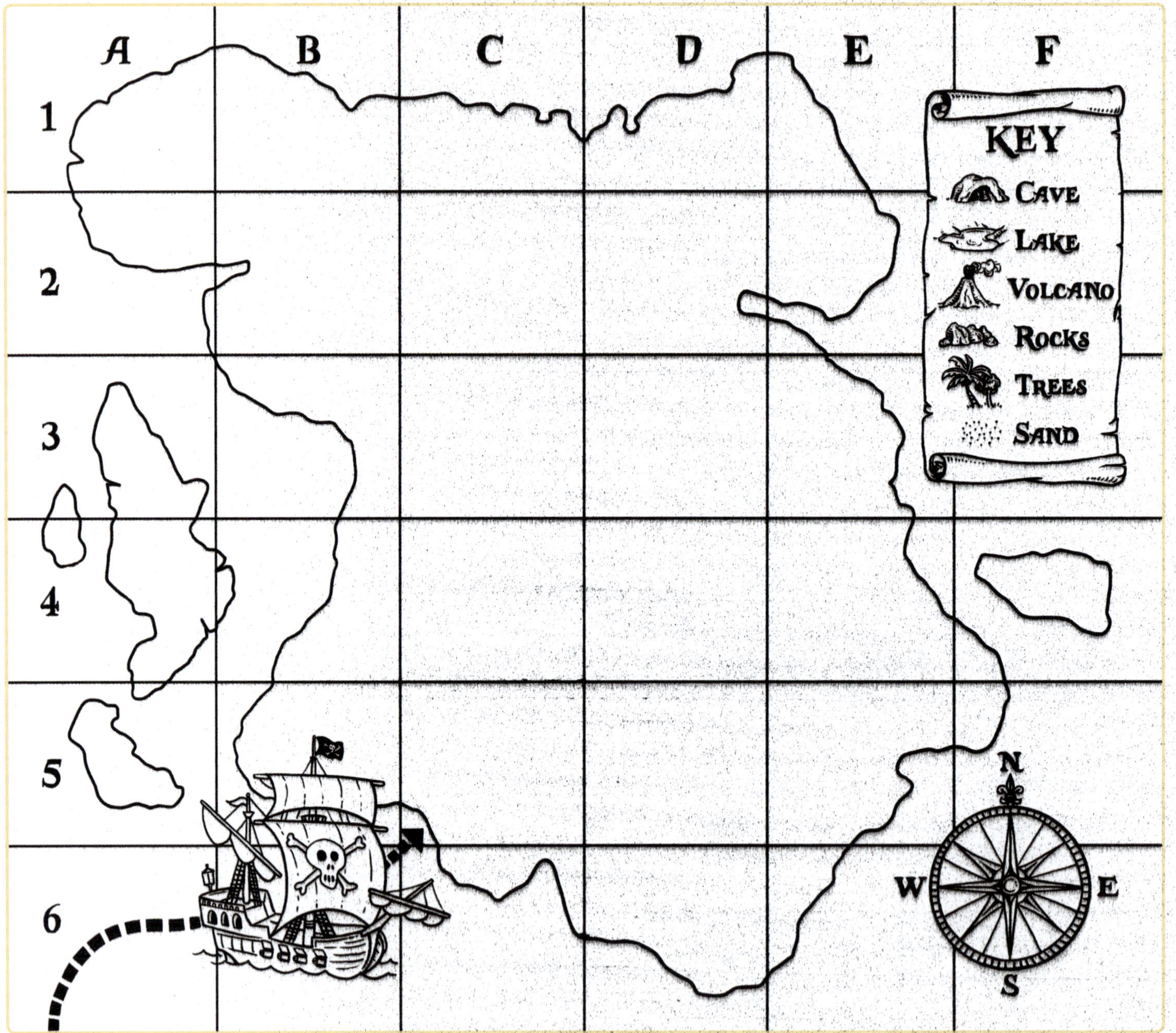

4 Activity 1

Treasure chest

Treasure chests are big and heavy and filled with gold! Make a treasure chest to scale. What are you going to put in your treasure chest?

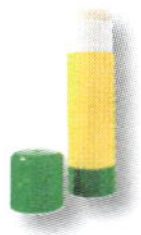

Step 1

Colour the chest.

Step 2

Press out the template.

Step 3

Fold the lines.

Step 4

Glue the treasure chest together.

Template **pages 67** and **69**

3 Lots of lines

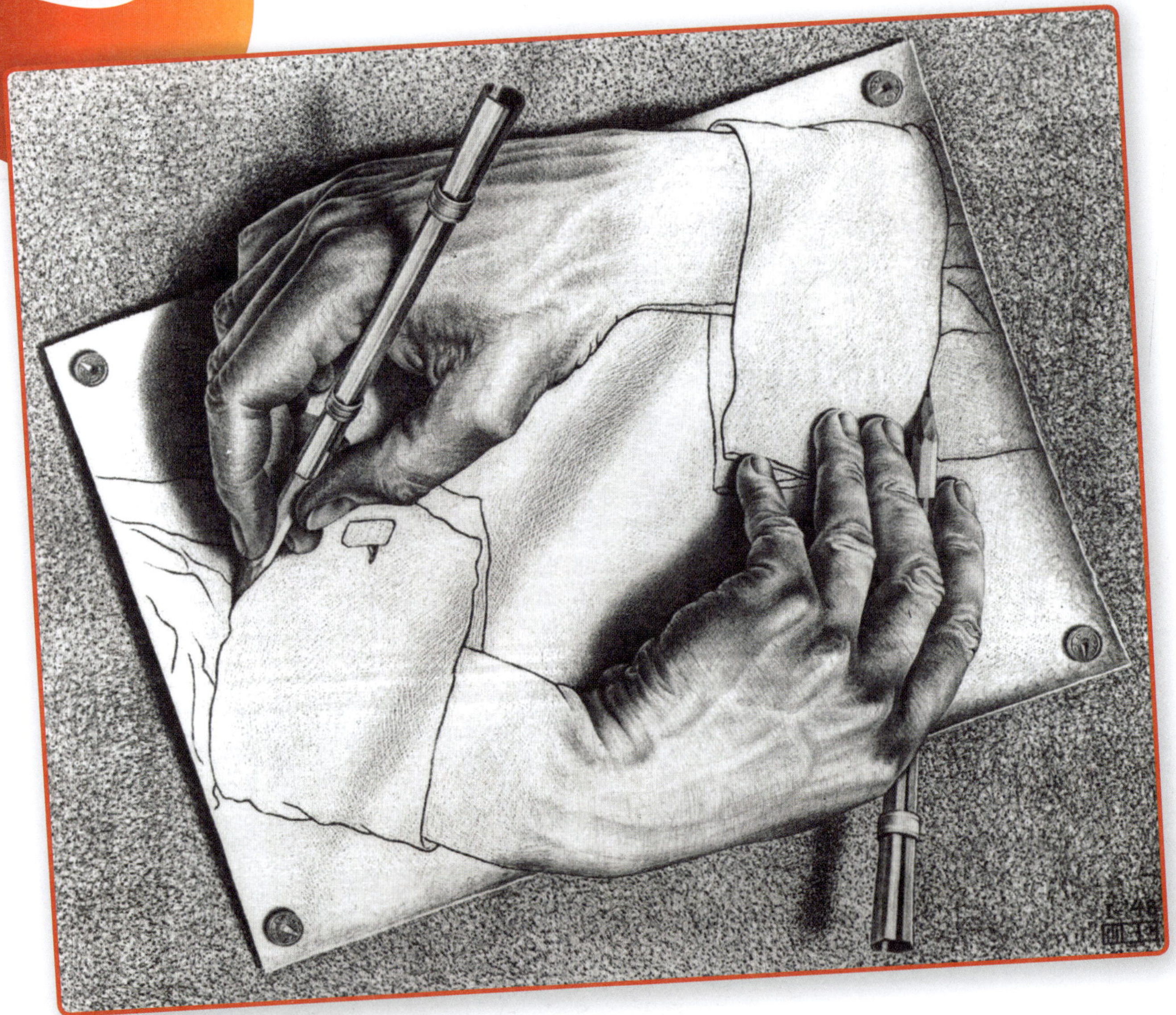

Drawing Hands, M.C. Escher. 1948

1 What are the hands in the artwork doing? Use the words below to help you.

button cuff pen sleeve three-dimensional wrist

2 Read about how artists make objects look three-dimensional.

Contour Lines

M.C. Escher uses contour lines to draw objects. Contour lines show the edges and the surface of an object. In this artwork, we can see two hands drawing contour lines to show the sleeves of a shirt.

To make an object look three-dimensional, artists draw the outline or edge of an object first. Then they add more contour lines inside the outline to show volume.

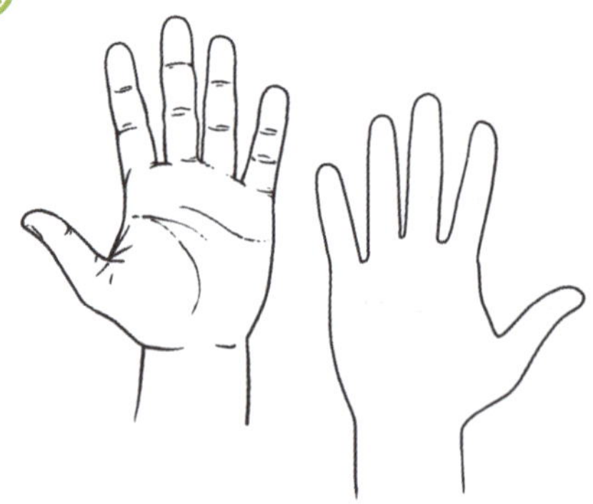

Which of these two hands looks three-dimensional? Why?

5 Activity 2

3 Complete the objects in the artist's sketchbook with contour lines. Draw an object from your classroom.

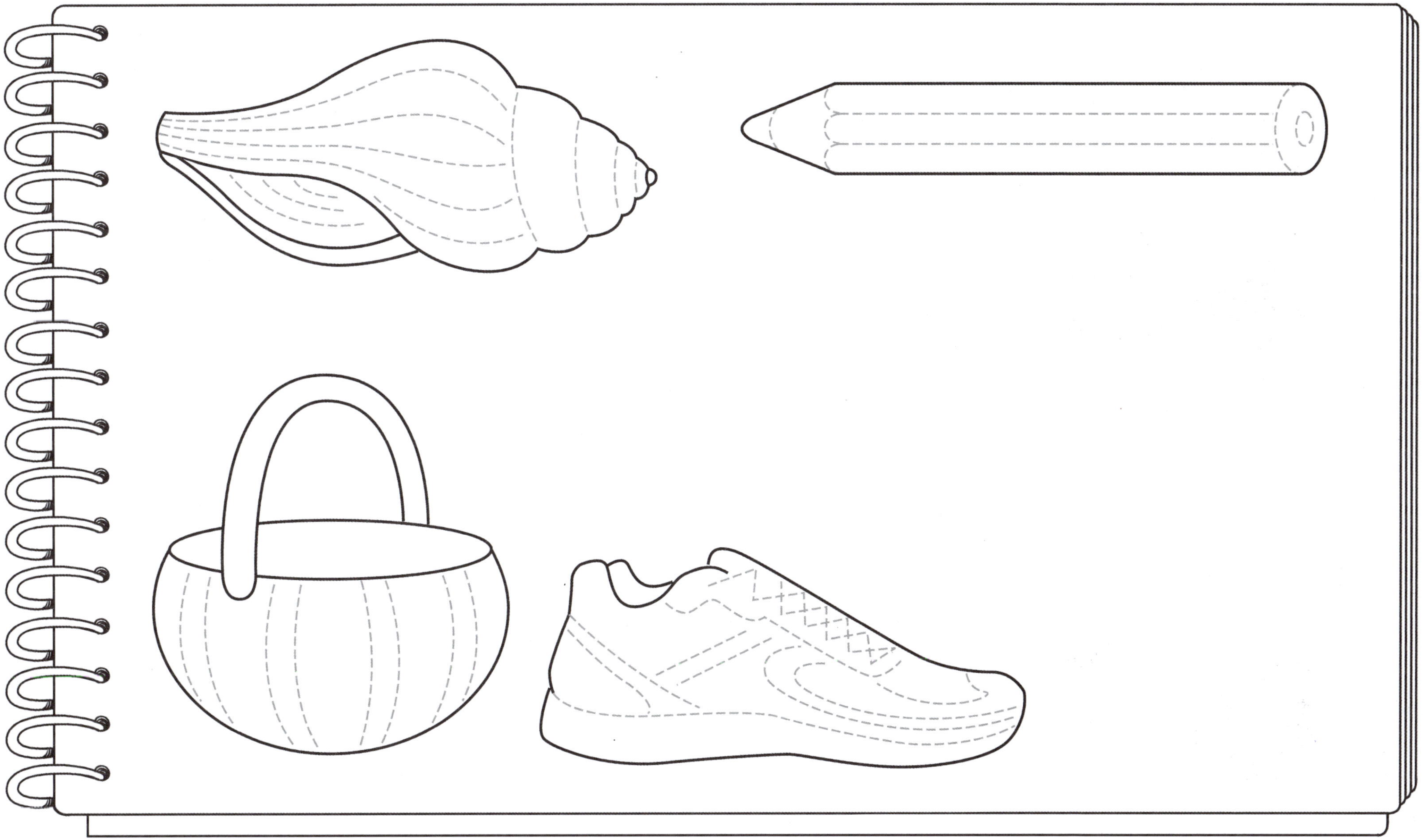

Use your eyes to draw

Artists follow the outline of an object with their eyes.
They let their eyes guide their hand.

1 Cut out a picture of an object from a magazine. Cut it in half. Glue.

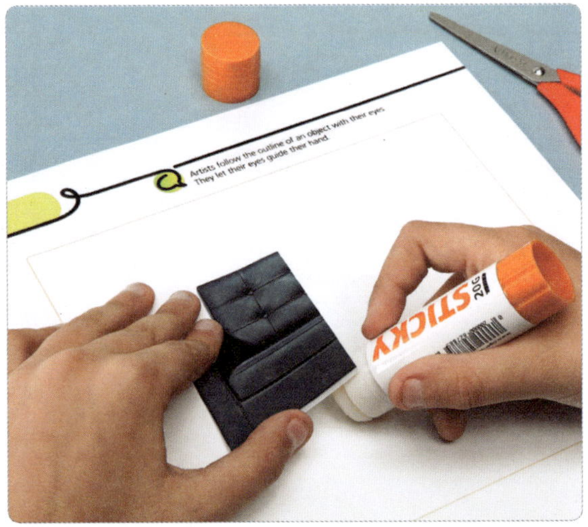

2 Complete the object using contour lines.

Surprising contours

Contour lines can be straight or curved, thick or thin. They can be different colours, too. Have fun with contour lines.

Step 1

Draw the outline of your hand and another object.

Step 2

Draw straight lines outside your outlines with colours.

Step 3

Draw curved lines with the same colours inside the outlines.

Step 4

Erase the pencil lines.

ART HISTORY 1 Prehistoric Art

La cueva de los caballos de Valltorta en Tírig (Castellón)

1 What does this cave art show us? Use the words below to help you.

arrow	bow	deer	herd	hunt	hunter

2 Read about how art can help us learn about prehistoric people.

Cave Art

Prehistoric people painted pictures in caves to tell stories or to show special events. The oldest examples of cave art have been found in hundreds of caves in Spain and France.

People painted pictures of animals. They often used the natural lines and bumps in the rock as contour lines in their artwork. This cave art also shows figures with long, thin bodies.

How do you think prehistoric people made paint for their artwork?

6 Activity 2

Rock texture

Most cave paintings are found deep inside caves in places that are difficult to find. People painted their images on the walls and ceilings of the cave.

Step 1

Crumple the paper. Open it carefully.

Step 2

Paint the paper brown.

Step 3

Add red, orange and yellow.

Step 4

Sprinkle salt on the wet paint.

Modern cave art

We can learn a lot about prehistoric people and their lives by looking at their art.
What can people learn about you by looking at your cave art?

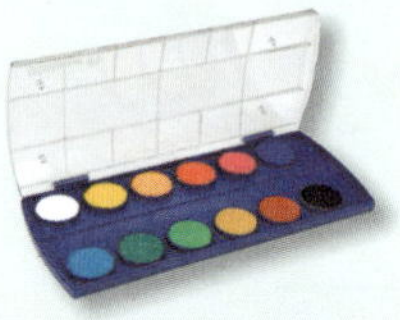

Work together
Invent a story using your cave paintings.

Step 5

Paint people and objects in black.

Step 6

Add colour.

Step 7

Cut the edges of your artwork.

Cave art in Spain

1 Listen to the information about cave paintings in the Altamira Cave. Tick the words you hear.

- [ ] north
- [ ] south
- [ ] 270 metres
- [ ] 370 metres
- [ ] bison
- [ ] elephants

2 Listen again and answer the questions.

1. Where is the cave?

   The Altamira cave is in ____.

2. How old are the cave paintings?

   The cave paintings are ____.

3. What images are there in this cave?

   In this cave there are images of ____.

3 Work in groups. Make a poster about prehistoric art in Spain.

[7] Activity 1 [8] Activity 2

4 Colours on parade

Mooquet, Terrell Powell. 2011

1 What can you see on the cow sculpture? Use the words below to help you.

dark	horns	light	line	pattern	shape

2 Read about how artists make colours lighter and darker.

Tints and Shades

This sculpture of a cow is part of the Cow Parade, an international art exhibit. Almost a hundred cities around the world have participated. Artists from each city paint their cow in their own unique way. This artist painted designs with lots of different colours.

Artists can make colours lighter by adding white; colours mixed with white are called tints. Artists can make colours darker by adding black; colours mixed with black are called shades.

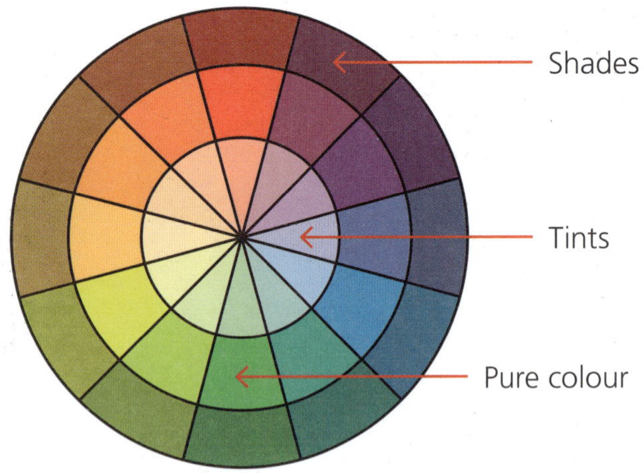

Find tints and shades of blue and red on the cow sculpture.

Activity 2

3 Find tints and shades of two different colours in a magazine. Cut out small pieces. Glue them on the cow in decorative patterns.

Monochrome designs

Some artworks are monochrome. They are made up of tints and shades of just one colour.

1. Use a black felt tip. Draw lots of different lines.

2. Choose a colour. Paint some of the spaces.

3. Paint the rest of the spaces with tints and shades.

Cow parade

The Cow Parades still continue today in different places around the world. You can create your own classroom cow parade.

Step 1

Trace the template shapes onto cardboard and cut them out.

Step 2

Colour both sides of the shapes.

Step 3

Add patterns with a white oil pastel.

Step 4

Put the pieces together.

Template page 71

5 Showing shadows

The Lorelei, Salvador Dalí. 1950

1 What shadows can you find in this artwork? Use the words below to help you.

background butterfly cave cliff flower foreground rock

2 Read about how artists show shadows.

Light and Shadows

Salvador Dalí painted interesting shadows in his artworks. Shadows are created when an object blocks a light source. In this artwork we can see the light source coming from the Sun in the sky. The flowers and butterflies block the light. You can see their shadows on the rock.

The size of a shadow changes with the position of the light source. A light source from above makes a smaller, shorter shadow. A light source from the side makes a bigger, longer shadow.

Look at the flowers. Which flower has got the longest shadow? Why?

10 Activity 2

3 Look at the example. Draw the shadows of the figures. Add details.

So many shadows

Artists can move the light source to change the shape and direction of a shadow.

1. Make a letter with plasticine.

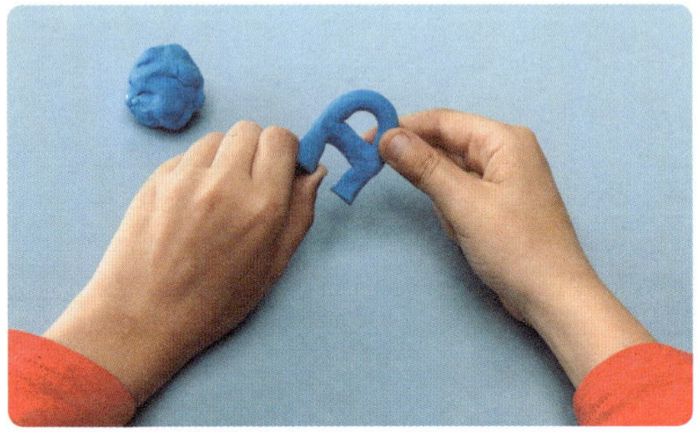

2. Point a torch at your letter. Draw the shadow.

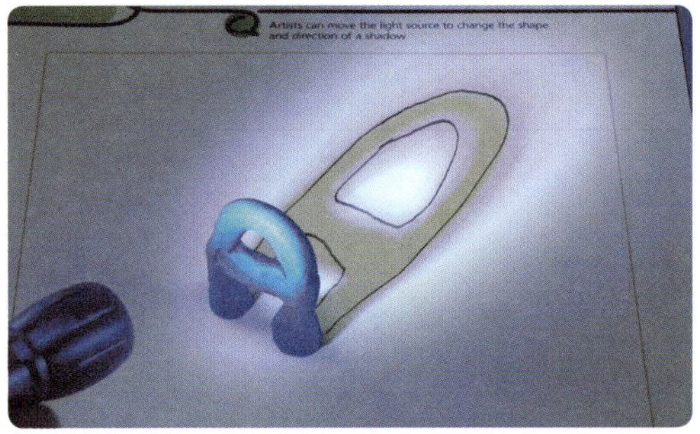

3. Move the light and repeat. Colour the shadows.

Shadow maker

When an object blocks light, a shadow is created. Shadows show the outline of the object and are usually dark, but you can make colourful shadows too.

Step 1

Cut out different shapes from cellophane.

Step 2

Make a pattern with the shapes.

Step 3

Glue the shapes onto the glass jar.

Step 4

Add a candle and turn off the lights.

6 Light and dark

Apples and Oranges, Paul Cézanne. 1895

1. Where can you see tints, shades and shadows in this still life? Use the words below to help you.

bowl   jug   pattern   plate   shadow   tablecloth

2. Read about how artists show volume in a still life.

Tints, Shades and Shadows

Paul Cézanne painted more than two hundred still life paintings. Cézanne used tints, shades and shadows to show volume in the objects he painted.

Artists paint tints to show the reflection of the light source. Then they paint shades to show the absence of light. Finally, they add a shadow to show where the light is blocked. Artists can shade in different ways. They can use dots, lines, smudges and colour.

Look at the photo. Where is the light source? How do you know?

11 Activity 2

3 Look at the photo and the example drawing. Draw the jug and use lines to shade. Look carefully at the light source.

Shading with colour

Artists gradually change from tints to shades to show volume. They use different shading techniques.

1. Colour the apple. Add tints and shades.

2. Colour the table. Add the shadow.

3. Colour the background.

Still life

Artists choose objects for a still life. They arrange them on a table and position their light source.

Step 1

Observe the objects on the table. Draw their outlines.

Step 2

Paint the objects. Add tints and shades.

Step 3

Paint the table and the shadows.

Step 4

Paint the background.

ART HISTORY 2 Roman Art

The Four Seasons. Floor Mosaic from the area of Le Capannelle, Rome. 4th-5th Century.

1. How are the four seasons represented in this mosaic? Use the words below to help you.

bird	crop	fruit	pattern	people

2. Read about Roman mosaics.

Roman Mosaics

The Romans decorated the floors of important buildings with mosaics. Many mosaics showed images of plants, animals and people. Some mosaics showed scenes from Roman mythology and history. Others represented daily life. This mosaic shows an image of the four seasons.

Each mosaic was made up of thousands of small pieces to show fine detail. The artists used tints and shades to show light and shadows.

How many small pieces do you think are in this mosaic fragment?

12 Activity 2

Plan your mosaic

Roman mosaics show images from nature including leaves, flowers, trees and animals. They made a border around the image with patterns.

Step 1

Work with your partner to plan your mosaic.

Step 2

Prepare your mosaic.

Step 3

Paint the pulses. Use tints and shades.

A mosaic calendar

Roman mosaics were made up of small coloured tiles called tesserae. The artists created images by placing the tesserae in cement.

Work together
Make a classroom calendar.

Step 4

Glue your image in the centre of your plate.

Step 5

Glue the background around the image.

Step 6

Glue the border around the edge of the plate.

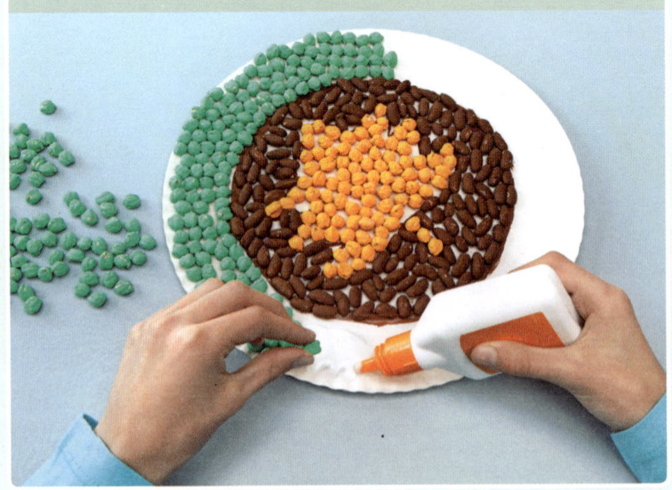

Roman mosaics in Spain

1 Listen to the information about a Roman mosaic in Spain. Tick the words you hear.

- [ ] story
- [ ] song
- [ ] strong
- [ ] weak
- [ ] deer
- [ ] horse

2 Listen again and answer the questions.

1. What is Roman mythology?

   Roman mythology tells stories about ______________________________
   ______________________________.

2. Where can we find images from Roman mythology?

   We can find images in ______________________________
   ______________________________.

3. What is Hercules doing in this mosaic?

   Hercules is capturing ______________________________
   ______________________________.

3 Work in groups. Make a poster about Roman art in Spain. Present your poster to the rest of the class.

13 Activity 1 14 Activity 2

7 Close up and far away

Plum Garden Kamata, Ando Hiroshige. 1857

1. What can you see in the background and middle ground of this landscape? Use the words below to help you.

blossom	grass	hut	lake	people	swing	tree

2. Read about how artists show depth in a landscape.

Positions in Space

The Japanese artist Ando Hiroshige shows depth in this landscape by placing objects in different positions in the space.

He painted many trees in this landscape. The first tree is placed at the bottom of the picture. It is the closest. The second tree is placed higher in the space. It is farther away. Finally, the trees in the background are smaller and placed even higher in the space. They look very far away.

Look at the arrows. What do you see at the bottom, in the middle and at the top of this photo?

15 Activity 2

3 Complete the Japanese landscape. Draw a rock in the foreground, a tree in the middle ground and another mountain in the background.

Silhouette landscape

Artists can combine colours and silhouettes to create a unique landscape with depth.

1. Colour the sky with warm colours. Blend the colours.

2. Cut out cool colours to make the land. Glue.

3. Cut out black silhouettes and glue them onto the landscape.

Print making

Hiroshige was an artist and a printmaker.
He cut his images of landscapes into wood.
Then he covered the image with ink
and pressed it onto paper to make a print.

Step 1

Design a foreground, middle ground and background.

Step 2

Cut the edges off the tray and etch your design.

Step 3

Paint the landscape. Keep the paint wet.

Step 4

Print the image onto paper.

8 Going, going, gone

Gran Vía, Antonio López. 1974-1981

1 How long do you think it took the artist to paint this cityscape? Use the words below to help you.

balcony	building	detail	realistic	street	window

2 Read about how artists paint realistic cityscapes.

Perspective Lines

Antonio López shows incredible details in his cityscapes. This painting of the Gran Vía in Madrid is very realistic and looks like a photo.

López uses a technique called perspective to show depth and volume in this cityscape. The buildings look three-dimensional and get smaller as they get further away. The two sides of the street get closer until they disappear at the vanishing point in the background.

Where can you see vertical, horizontal and diagonal lines in the illustration?

16 Activity 2

3 Trace the example. Follow the steps to draw simple city streets with volume and depth.

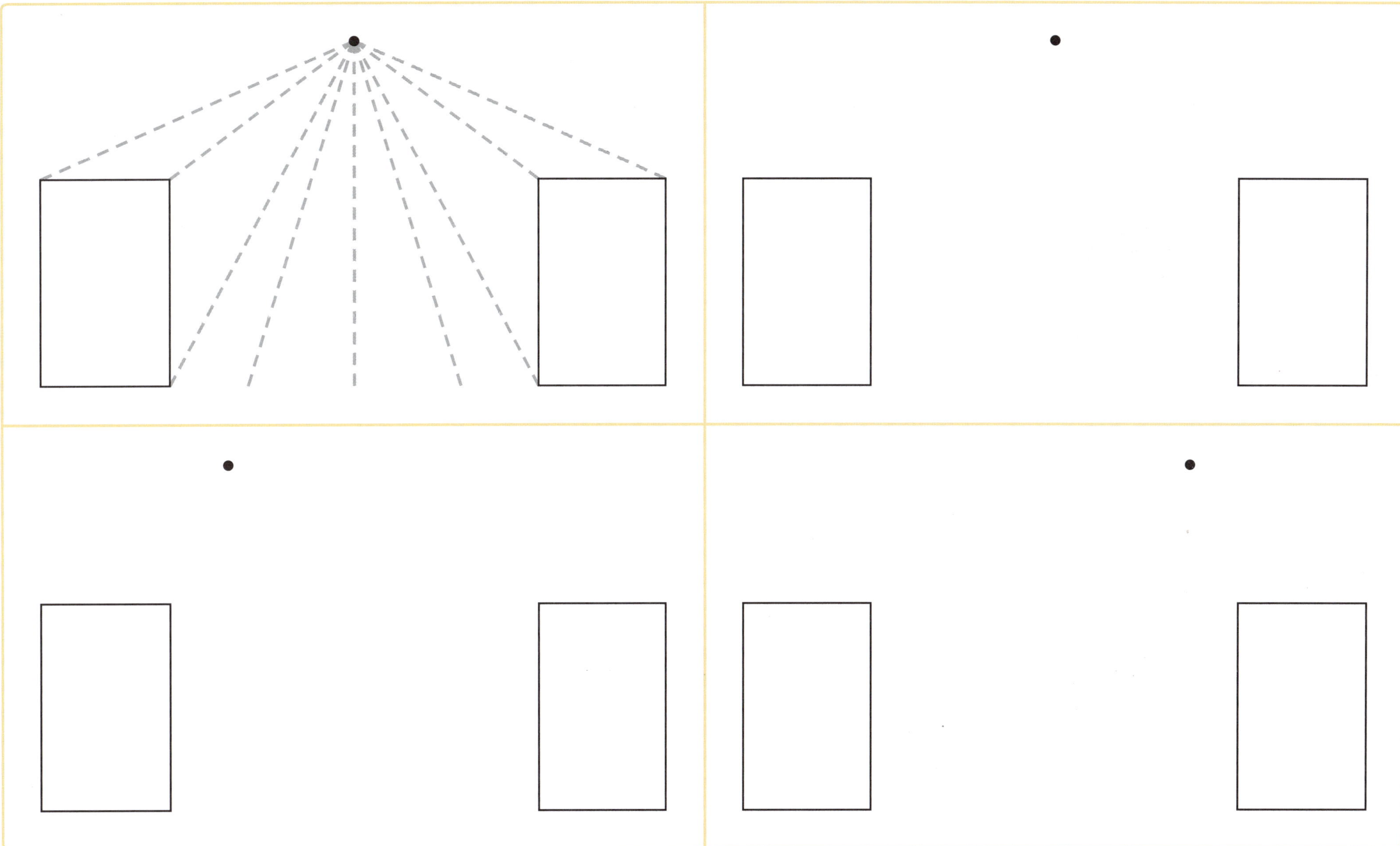

Lines in a city

To show depth in a cityscape, artists begin by drawing diagonal lines to a point in the distance called a vanishing point.

1. Look carefully at the diagonal, horizontal and vertical lines. Draw buildings on the other side of the street.

2. Draw windows and doors. Add details. Colour.

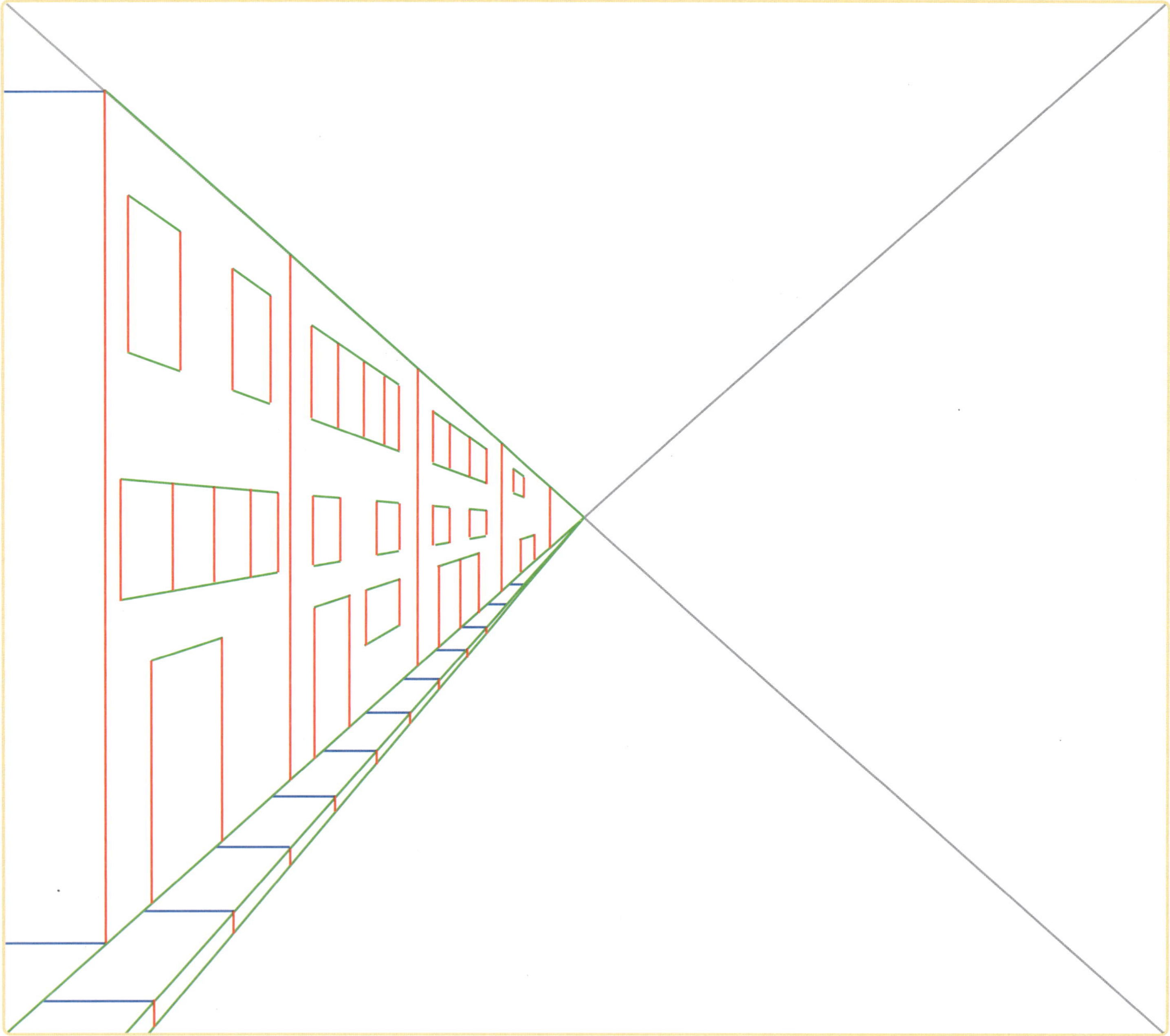

City street

Artists can create the illusion of depth and volume in a city street. They start with a vanishing point and then add lines, details and colour.

Step 1

Draw buildings.

Step 2

Add windows and doors.

Step 3

Add details.

Step 4

Colour.

Template page 73

9 Points of view

Sun on the pool, David Hockney. 1982

1 What can you see in this artwork? Use the words below to help you.

chair | diving board | palm tree | umbrella

2 Read about how artists use different points of view.

Points of View

David Hockney is a British artist. In some of his artworks he uses a camera to take photos of objects from different points of view.

In this artwork he took many photos and put them together like a collage. Hockney took photos of the swimming pool from above, which is called a bird's eye view. You can see that Hockney also took photos of objects from the side and added them to the artwork to create an unusual view of the swimming pool.

When have you seen something from a bird's eye view?

17 Activity 2

3 Draw a beach from a bird's eye view and a worm's eye view. Look at the words in the box to help you.

a beach ball	an umbrella	a bird	people	table and chairs	a sandcastle

Up, down and around

Photographers can take photos from different points of view. Use your detail detector like a view finder of a camera.

1 Observe your object from different points of view. Choose the angle you want to draw.

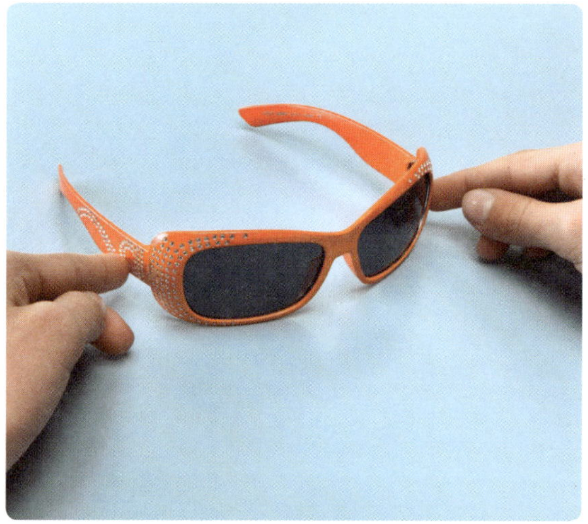

2 Draw the outline of your object. Add lines and details. Colour.

Two points of view

Photographers observe the world around them and take photos from different points of view. Artists can also show creative points of view in their drawings and paintings.

Step 1

Draw an object from different points of view.

Step 2

Cut out the lines.

Step 3

Glue in order. Fold.

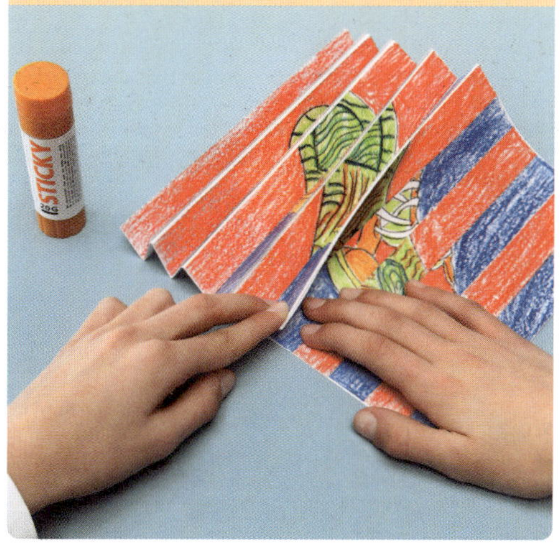

Step 4

Look at your artwork from opposite points of view.

Template **page 75**

ART HISTORY 3 Medieval Art

Painting of the port of Naples, San Martino Museum.

1 What can you see in this painting? Use the words below to help you.

castle	harbour	hill	ship	tower

2 Read about how medieval castles were designed.

Medieval Castles

Castles in the Middle Ages were designed for fortification and protection. Most castles had a large entrance called a gate house, a central courtyard and a main tower called a keep. High, thick walls with towers surrounded these structures. Some castles were built on a hill so that the guards could look in all directions for enemies. Other castles had a dry moat or a moat filled with water that went all around the castle walls for extra protection.

Can you name the different parts of the castle in the illustration?

18 Activity 2

Design and construct a castle

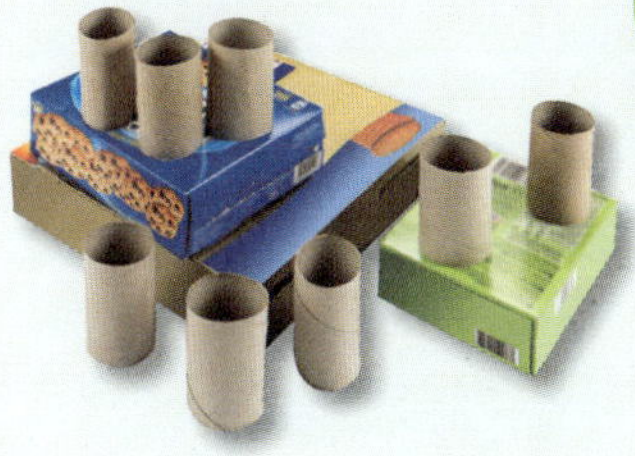

Medieval castles were built from stones or mud bricks. Some castles had a very basic, functional design. Other castles were decorated with elaborate details.

Step 1

Design your castle.

Step 2

Cut the different parts of your castle.

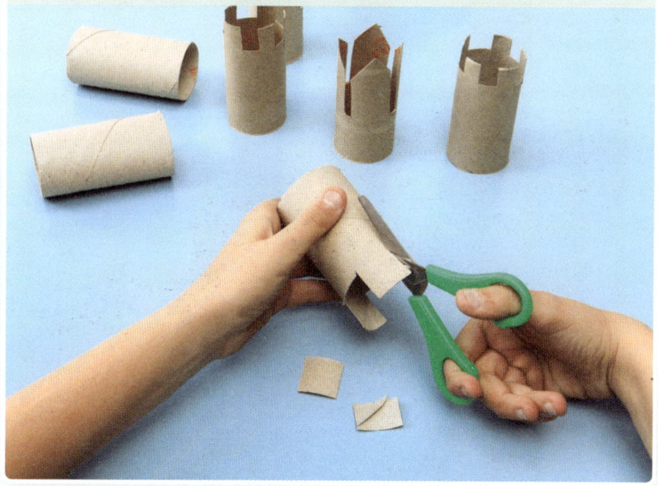

Step 3

Glue it together. Hold each object while the glue dries.

My castle

Today, many books, films and artworks show castles as magical places filled with princesses, knights and dragons. What kind of castle will yours be?

Work together
Invent a story using your castle.

Step 4

Paint your castle.

Step 5

Add details.

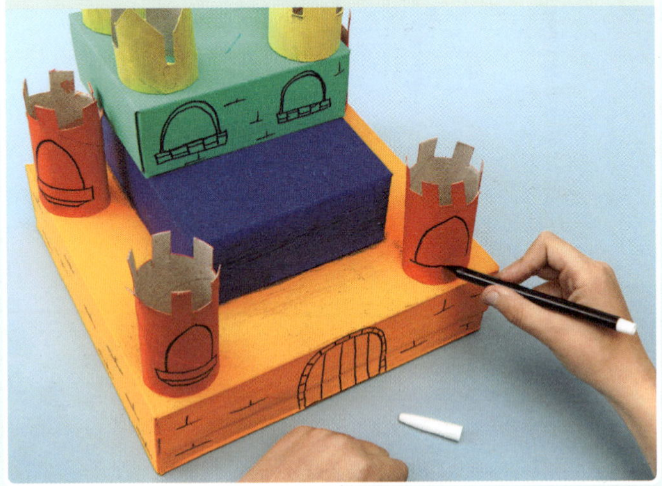

Step 6

Decorate the area around your castle.

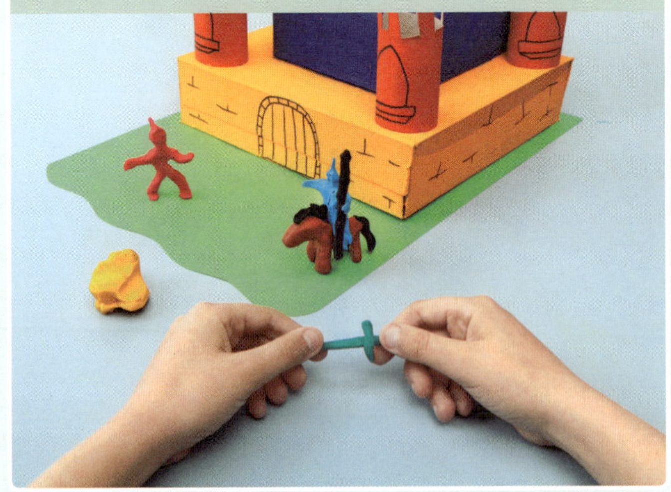

Castles in Spain

1 Listen to the information about a medieval castle in Spain. Tick the words you hear.

- ☐ frontier
- ☐ valley
- ☐ rocky
- ☐ flat
- ☐ tower
- ☐ garden

2 Listen again and answer the questions.

1. Where is the castle?

   ____

   ____.

2. When was it built?

   ____

   ____.

3. What are some important parts of the castle?

   ____

   ____.

3 Work in groups. Make a poster about medieval art in Spain. Present your poster to the rest of the class.

19 Activity 1 20 Activity 2

Winter decoration

It's winter time and snow falls in many places around the world. Children enjoy making snowmen and snowballs for snowball fights. Make a winter ball decoration!

Step 1

Inflate a small balloon.

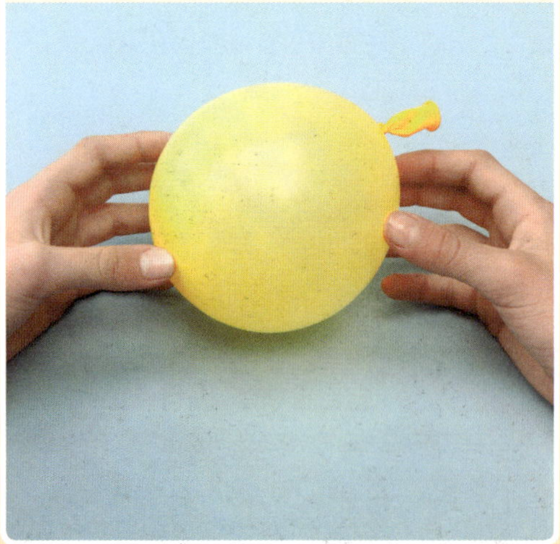

Step 2

Cover the wool in glue.

Step 3

Wrap the wool around the balloon.

Step 4

Let the wool dry. Pop the balloon.

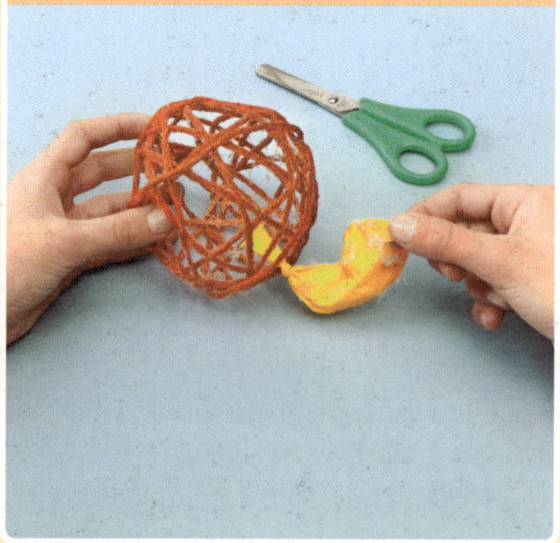

Christmas cracker

Christmas is a special time for family and friends. It is celebrated in different ways in different parts of the world. Make a Christmas cracker. It is a colourful tube with a special note and a present inside.

Step 1

Write and decorate a Christmas note.

Step 2

Put the note and a present inside the tube.

Step 3

Glue tissue paper around the tube.

Step 4

Tie two ribbons on each end and decorate.

Shadow play

Puppets are used to tell stories. People from China use shadow puppets. They shine a light on their puppet to create a shadow on a white screen.
You can make a traditional Chinese dragon puppet. Make a shadow play with friends to celebrate World Theatre Day.

Step 1

Fold the strips of paper. Connect the pieces.

Step 2

Colour, press out and glue the front and back of the dragon.

Step 3

Glue two sticks to your puppet.

Step 4

Use a torch to see your shadow puppet.

Template page 77

Spring flowers

Spring is the season of new life. The weather gets warmer and the days get longer.
The leaves grow on the trees and the flowers begin to bloom.

Step 1

Fold the card.
Draw the outline of a flower.

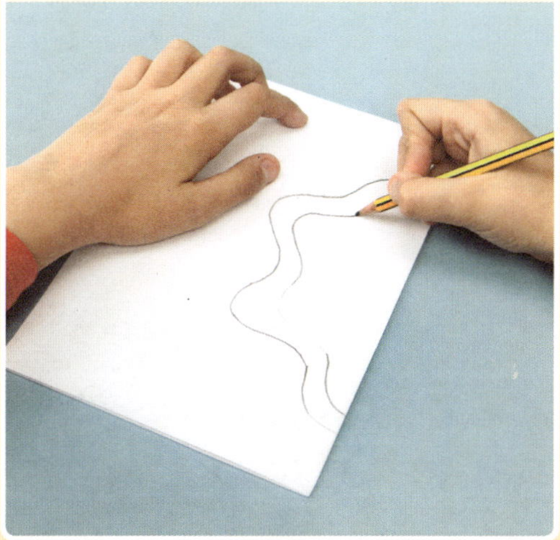

Step 2

Cut out the flower and stick it on contact paper.

Step 3

Add small pieces of cellophane.

Step 4

Stick it to a window to catch the spring sunlight.

Wild about reading

World Book Day is celebrated on 23 April. It is a special day to promote reading and writing. Books are filled with adventure, fantasy, laughter and emotion. Find a book today and start reading!

Step 1

Fold and glue side B to side A.

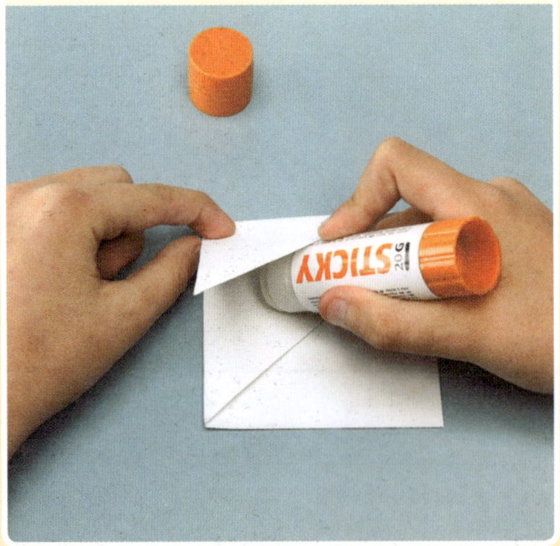

Step 2

Colour.

Step 3

Add eyes and a mouth.

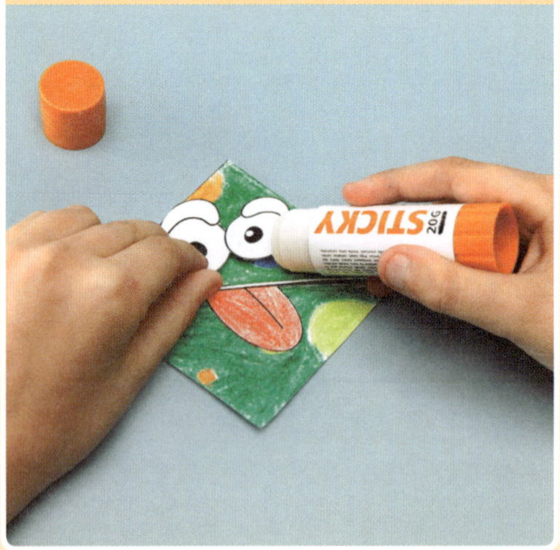

Step 4

Use it as a bookmark.

Template page 79

World Music Day

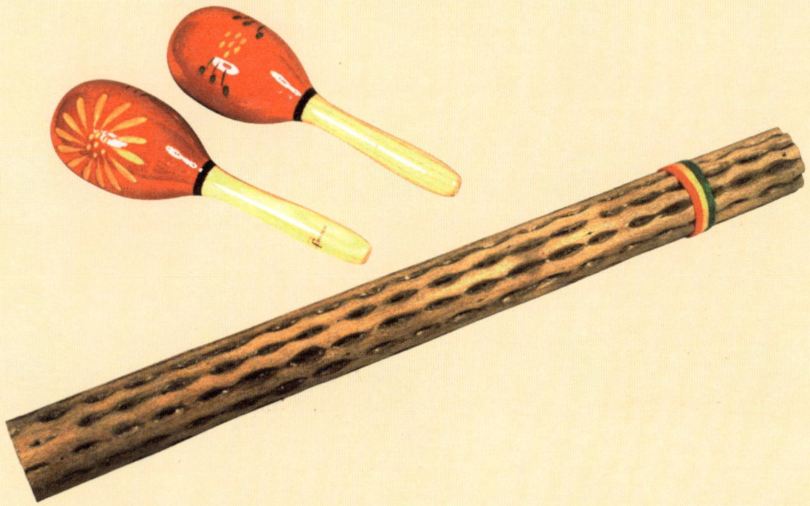

People make music everywhere in the world. They sing in different languages and use different types of instruments.

A rain stick is a special instrument used in rain ceremonies in many different countries. Musicians sing and dance and play the rain stick to make a soft sound like rain.

Step 1

Cut and glue paper on one end of the tube.

Step 2

Twist tin foil into long spirals.

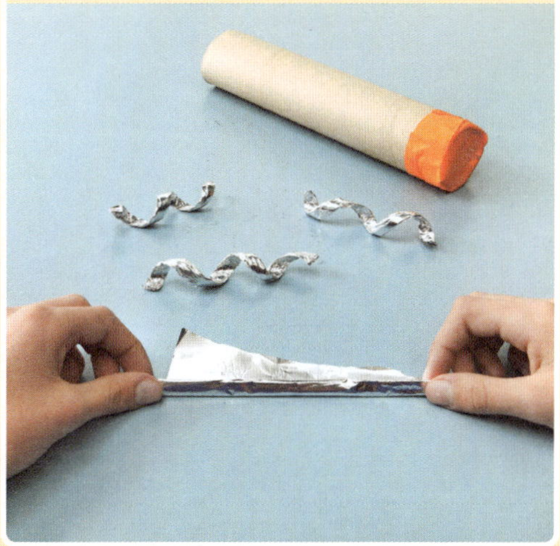

Step 3

Put the tin foil and rice inside the tube.

Step 4

Glue paper to the other end and decorate your rain stick.

Describe

What can you see in the artwork?

I can see animals, buildings, food, people, plants, etc.

It's a ...

painting

sculpture

mosaic

print

Respond

What does the artist show?

What does the artwork make you think about?

The artist shows children playing together.

It makes me think about summer.

Analyse

What did the artist use?

lines

shapes

patterns

colours

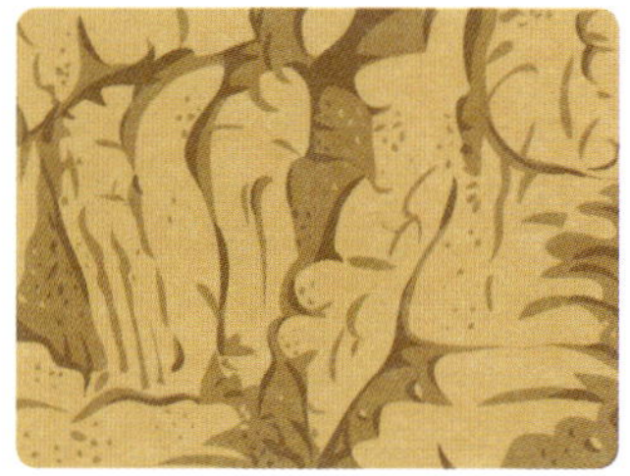

textures

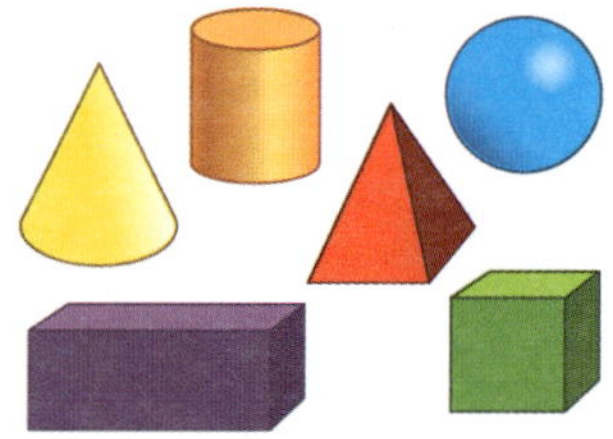

forms

Evaluate

What's your opinion of the artwork?

What do you like about the artwork?

It's interesting.
It's funny.

I like the different patterns.
I don't like the dark colours.

Paper

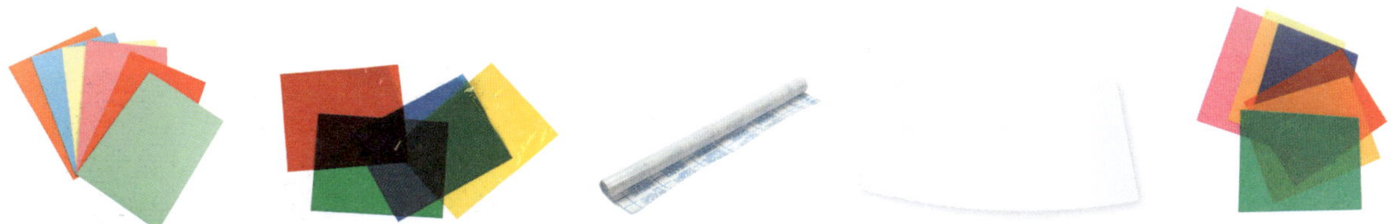

card, cellophane paper, contact paper, paper, tissue paper

Glue

glue stick, white glue

Mould

plasticine

Cut

scissors

Draw and colour

coloured pencils, crayons, felt tips

oil pastels, pencil, permanent marker

Paint

paintbrush, poster paint, water, watercolours

Extra materials

aluminium foil, balloons, boxes, cardboard, compass

glass jar, magazine, pulses, punch, paper plate

paper roll, pencil sharpener, polystyrene tray, recycled materials, rubber

ruler, set squares, sticks, torch, wool

Contour lines

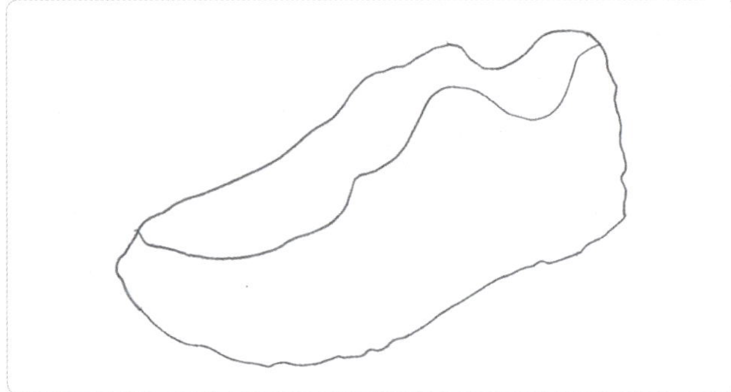

Draw the outline of the object.

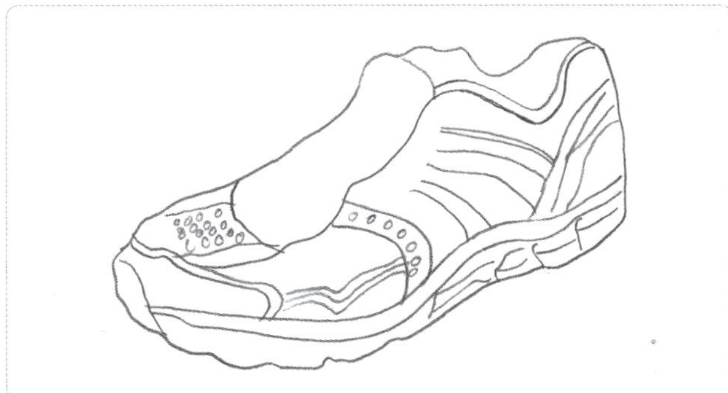

Add more contour lines inside the outline.

Add details.

Tints

Choose a colour. Add white to make a tint. Add more white to make the tint lighter.

Shades

Choose a colour. Add black to make a shade. Add more black to make the shade darker.

Volume

Draw an object. Colour the object with one colour.

Choose a light source. Colour the area near the light with tints.

Colour the area far from the light with shades.

Add a shadow opposite the light source.

Space

Draw a horizon line high up on the paper. Draw objects in the foreground near the bottom.

Draw objects that are far away smaller and higher on the paper.

Add other objects near and far. Colour.

Depth

Draw a horizon line. Add a vanishing point.

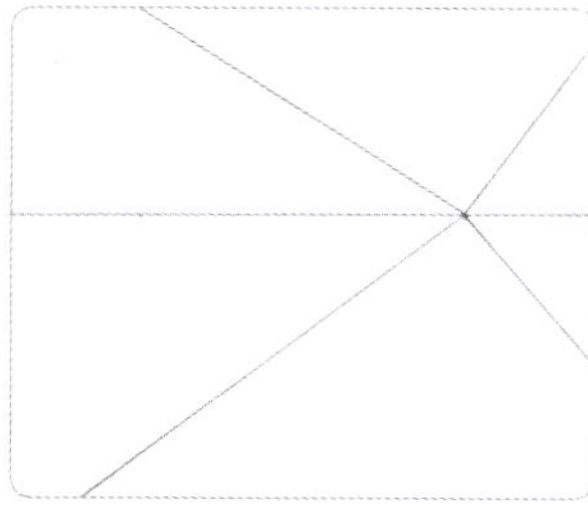

Draw four diagonal lines from the vanishing point.

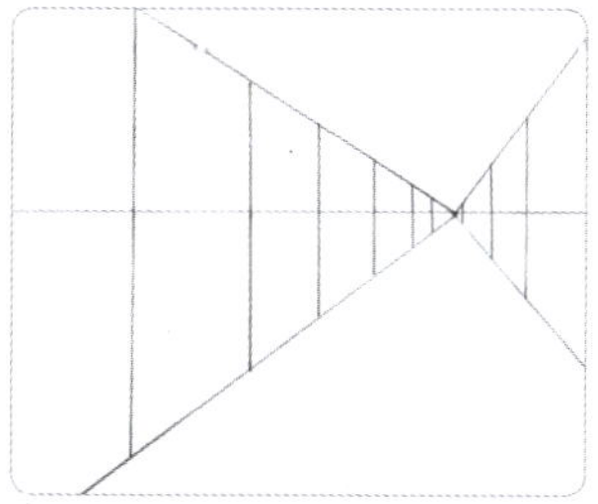

Draw vertical lines to make the buildings.

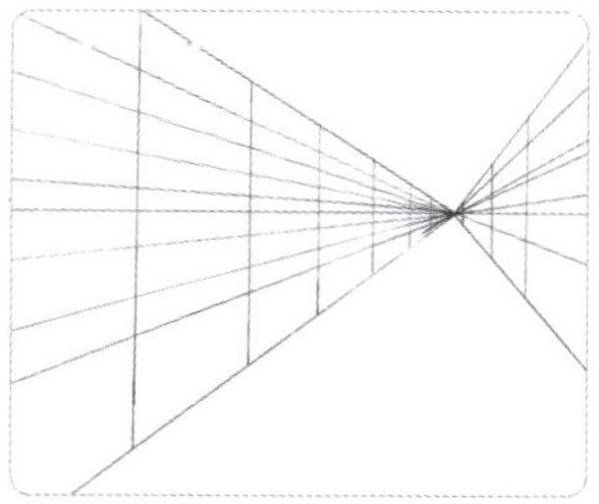

Draw more diagonal lines from the vanishing point.

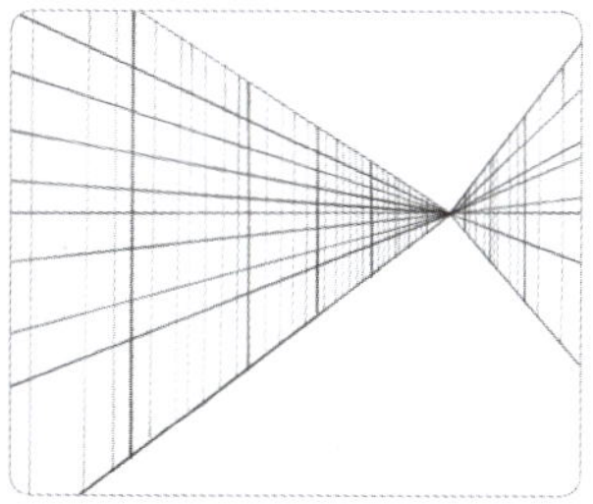

Draw vertical lines for the windows and doors.

Add more diagonal lines for the street. Erase the extra lines, add details

Points of view

Bird's eye view

Worm's eye view

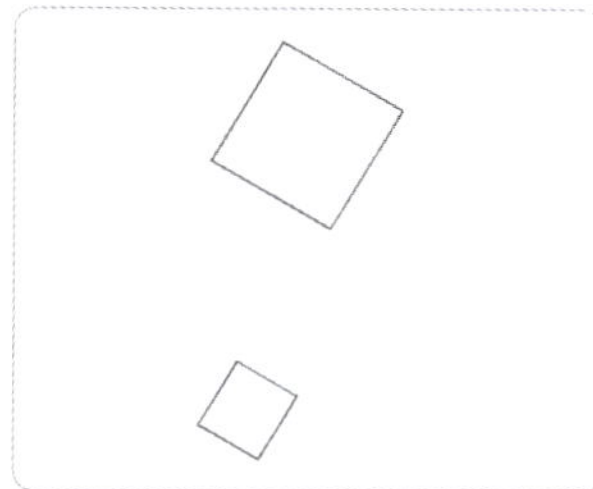

Draw a large shape at the top and a smaller shape at the bottom.

Draw a small line at the top and a bigger line at the bottom.

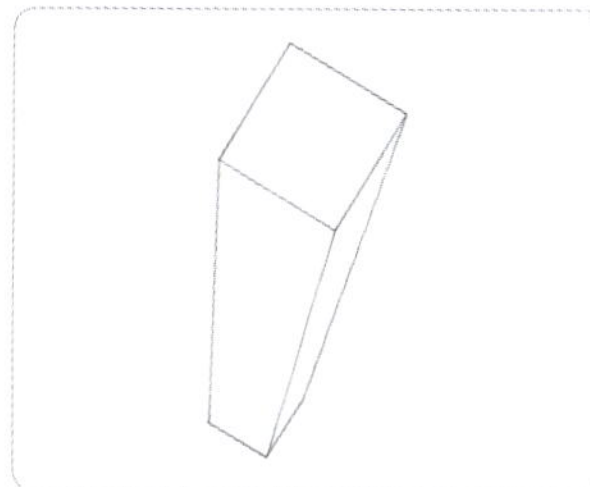

Draw lines to connect the corners. Erase the invisible lines.

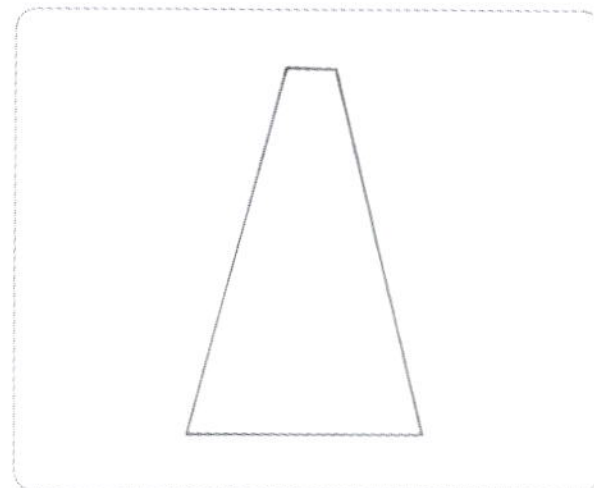

Connect the two lines.

Add details that get smaller at the bottom.

Add details that get smaller at the top.

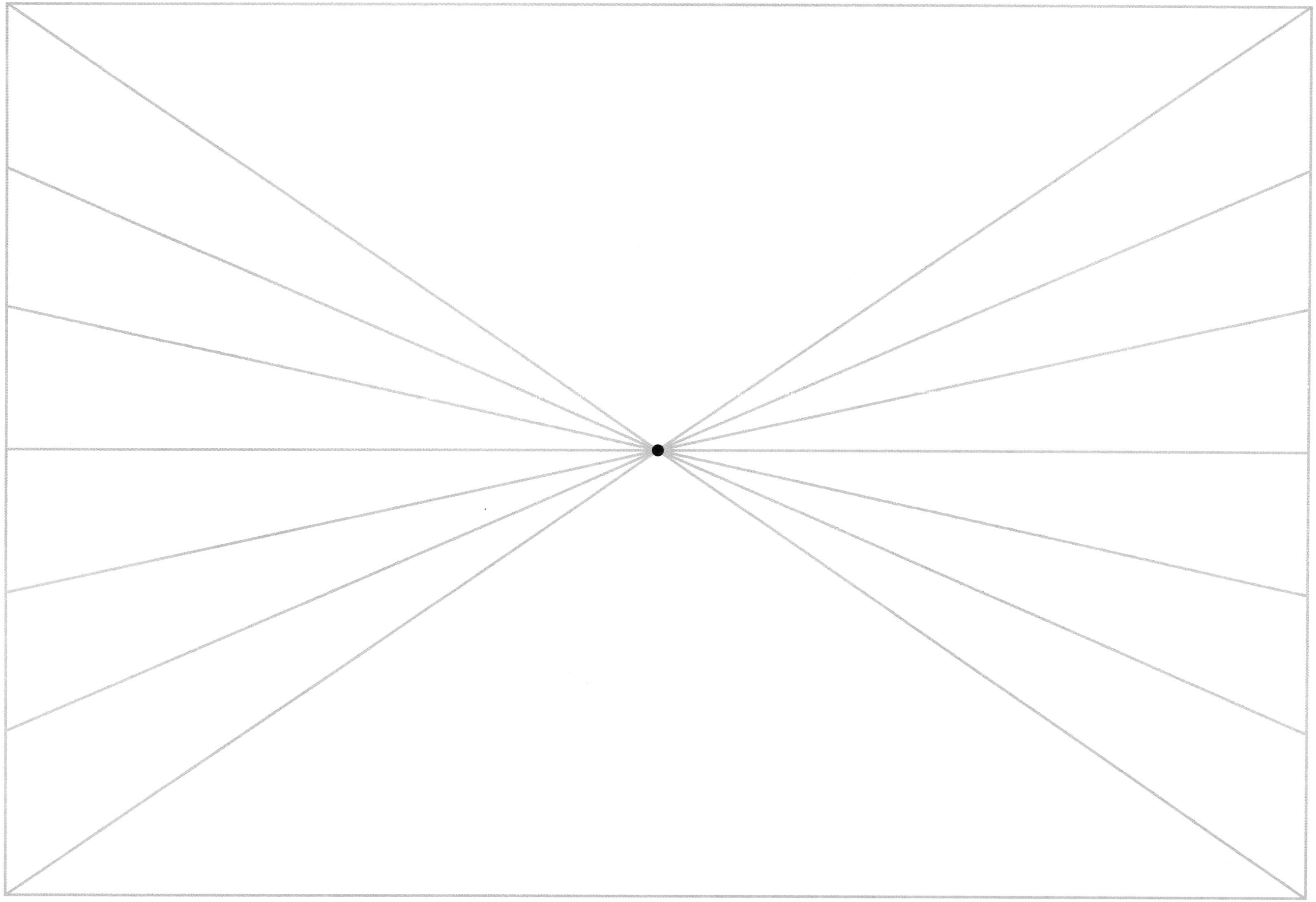

A

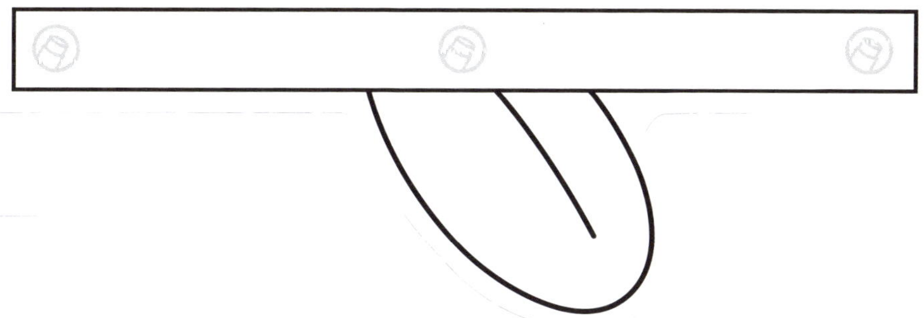

B

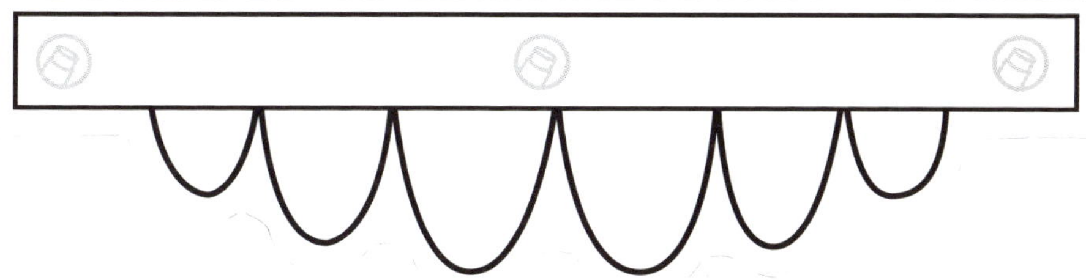